AF610473

Published by lulu.com

ISBN 978-0-557-06911-8

1 2 3 4 5 6 7 8 9 0

Casa de Cuerva

Ethan Applegarth

501 Poems

Dedicated to my sister Claire

"En tanto que de rosa y azucena
Se muestra la color en vuestro gesto,
En vuestro mirar ardiente, honesto,
Enciende al corazon y lo refrena."
Garcilaso de la Vega (1501-1536), SONETO XXIII

1

Human objects course the sky
Madly wing it elsewhere
And miss the torrid speed
Of dragonflies borne on the breeze

2

GATHERING WOOD

There is a certain Zen about wood gathering
That branch: too wild and twisted
That one: too delicate to take
This: too close to home
That other: too alone, too much in its own place
All wood's too good to take
Each year a fresh crop of wood
Each year new decisions made

3

The beetle on its back
Amid the mountain-grains
Will get a little finger
Of intervention

4

Under the great *palo verde*
The wash sounds with cricket depth
The outer eye drifts
Into dream time

5
The old pale moon
Wearily wears a way
Over the knob of the hill
Wears the turning earth

6
Wander under far country
Fire burns bright between boulders
Curl to the flames
Touch an image of melted glass
This is what it means to be free
Lost amid a forest of hollow trunks
The clean road whispers, beckons under the crystal ceiling
You shall ride and tomorrow there shall be high rafters
Lost cities of the plain, beaded peacocks
And stranger women than the world has ever seen

7
NARWHAL
He drank the word, swilled it in his mouth
Tasted a long-connoitered dead language
Which had crept out of Europe lusting wine
Now here in the wild, like a wayward gull, he charts a sea unknown to his ancestors

8
Like an ogre he sings down the trail
A tide of wild things flees
He stops to urinate, laughing
The proud beast of giant country

9

The track jumps a level, washbed style
Buddhist stones sit in the way with
Tire markings on their heads and
Pieces of blasted tailpipe offerings

10

MONOLITH

The great valley monolith
Marked by eons of native tongues
Bowed markings, tooled incisions, and flailing stick figures
Marching into the deeps of time
Stands at the confluence of gathering-trails
As a god would pause and pass into dreamlands undiscovered
X-ray turtles crisscross its back
Shadow shamans drum its knees
The wilds encroach and cover its flanks with hairy bristles
As seasons, like breaths, dip high and low below the horizon

11

A bush, backcountry, outback, desert rat ruin
Just a sign shot through
'Do not—' all that is left
Fill in the blank and be on the way

12

He walks a ruined way
Foreign cat's eyes on the back of his neck
Through groves of trickling witchery
His course a wooded neck

13
IN THE PLACE OF THE DEAD
In the depths of the bag one night
A *nachtmusik* of stars rained down, and
Spectral figures of the stones, such
Haloed native harbingers came from
Amidst the burning grounds

14
Camp is far away and night is falling in
So like a hunted hare I vault the bracken
Wade in stone fields up to my waist
Pull at the crumbling washsides—
Finger ledges molded in sun-soaked brine—
The avian chorus fades
Then at the rise, the zenith, a dozen, two dozen valleys more
It will be a thirsty evening
And a feeling-out across pale arroyos
Thick in fading dusk

15
The red-crested woodpecker swept low
I lay still
He, intent to create understanding
Chopped a branch, looked my way

16
Stardown on the summit
Breath of the night
I, wrapped in white sheets
Listen to my ears

17
VIVA EL CAZADOR
I laid crosshairs on the rabbit's back and felt him drain away
He feasted on low branches while I counted time for him to flee
At last the bullet broke him and I rose and paced his way
Viva el cazador

18
Year of the field mice
In cupboards, under the floor
I have no answers
Cheese licked off, traps unsprung

19
Closing year and
The light fades quickly
Distant ridge
Smoke in weltered air

20
Mexico was guitars and clipped roses
Los momentos felices
She brushed my hand, eyes startled
I gave my blood, my highest anima
Something ethereal crept inside
And we danced the moon away
From what deep reaches did she come?
An innermost hold of waving beauty
Her wise straight path, unyielding to my door

21
ESPALDA REINA
Horizons are subsumed
And I have been retaken
Fallen to earth
It is a new world
I wash myself
Stretch white hands to face
Gasp in the waters
Oye, mamá
Ya pagé el diablo
Now I am released
Upon an unsuspecting world
I hold keys to your resuscitation
Stolen from benighted *mar*
Tangle with me through the thick
Toss loose sheets to the wind
One can fall so far
One can fall from the heavens
In a worldly fallow moment
Yet the surface lies near
And the tide rushes in
Now we turn round and round
In dawn-tossed turmoil
Purple froth spews from the sea
As lamps wink out below blue horizon
Feed on feasts of fish

22
Coming home under open stars
Making footprints
Dark freedom of the hills
Un amor que crece trescientos veces

23
With me you'll find adventure
La lucha buena, amor puro
Caricias de inmortalidad
Pulsing heat beneath high palms

24
First footfalls
Of the great journey recede
Hills open, alive
With courteous attention

25
Ebb'ed light plays
And failed gloaming
Swirls to earth
Silence upcanyon way

26
Past solid-embraced cliffs
Rock-walled encroaching darkness
The way
Scattered bone-twigs

27
Wrought frail, the
Lavender stone falls unaware
To a sandy landing
I, intent, teeter on wash drafts

28
SPATULA
Open the packet
Spring one egg from its shell
Then two, mix
Beat, pour on hottened iron
Scrape, stay the edges
Lay the spatula down
And cherish its name
'Spatula', spatoola,
Queen of eggs
I love your regal bearing
High-necked
Long fluted body
Delicate handle
Never meant to touch
The heat
Maybe I should
Sit stilly outside
Beneath tethered stars in
Autumn morning darkness

29
Wishing-well smoke unrolls with
Resounding brightness
Succulent heat
The trail fire collapses inward

30
Clenched, comic jawed
He bit the cheroot stogie
Ceegar smoke washed his eyeballs
He strove to pierce wayward dark with eyes akimbo
Smoky fire
Glow-dark blues on the land

31
Bacon, egg whites, a crust of grainy bread
A camp morning cooking mess, this
Dead smoke, pit flames gurgle,
Tobacco juice, coffee grounds, gravel and sweat

32
After a half-night of words and drizzle
Two friends find silence
Wash the fire smoke from their hair
Drink a last cup and to bed

33
Like rolled trunks
Greasy with anticipation
The panified eggs congeal
Jellily mist into smoke

34
In the night-falling country, one star flutters overhead
I stalk blind ways, wide-eyed, feeling
But trees conspire, they direct me to
Formless outcrops, witch-spider country

35
Pensar de oblivion
Do stones, heated, feel?
Lustrous days imbecilic
Sate a sun symbolic

36
SEPTEMBER
Snake-eye stars wilt
The beholden road winds away
In inner dawn and branch country
A humid blanket of *oscuridad*

37
Dance of the wailing gargoyles
I ask, but humans are unwelcome
The Valley of Shades
House of the bone-pit and moon-glazed arbor

38
Ashen faced, play
Native ritual with lute and drums
Beat out the bird dance
Pour humanness into the sand

39
The horned moon sinks spent
And mountains take her
Hide her soon
False antidawn begone
And whalebone hills
Unmoored, floating
Stand out from starry shore
Begin the epic journey

40
Cicadic might beneath the mesquite tree
Bespread limbs
Dash succulent sound
Insectoid bodies gyrate together

41
Goodbye lilting Orion
Your belt is left on the mountain
Amongst cool rushes
Black flakes of the wash

42
I crossed the anthill, an
Obliterated pyramidal sepulcher
Volcanic rimmed,
Pharaonic generations, brief, built upward

43
Silent in the night
Dead radio pulses
Stars slide darkly by
Scudding remnants flee west

44
Burnt iris pierced with destitution
Night-eyed bonfire
Sallow moon-play has fled
And rising hills flicker

45
Ring around the moon
White rosie
Ushers deadened milk
To abandoned arroyos
Far and beyond pale sight
Murmurs the sand

46
Coyote, the Old Monk
Wears a cowl of matted grey
Bleary-eyed in the ocotillos
He treads the rising path
And with gentle paw
Mulls long scent
Squints into *paztiempo*
Continues up the way

47
At a point between kneeling and drinking
Feel the sky pour down
For heaven's no higher than grasses
Pressed by bended knee

48
Through star-swept places of peace
And emberic wind-on-the-fire
An unlikely homecoming
Whiff of crushed jasmine and mustard

49
Curs'ed years, walls tumble, split
Phrases lost to owners roam wild
Rats chew through historic words
And from architecture of rung tones
History rehashes the world
In wide untrammeled spaces
Secret fingers of humanism totter away
To strand us leeward to darkling plains

50
Is it wind or is that
The stones' rollicking
In the swift stream
Where the willows play?

51
Bloodshot eyes in coffee do no harm
Yet shield sweet discoveries
In the taunting morning light
Pink, brisk and calm

52
In the broken baroque grove
Skeletons dance on wings of eve
Their shrine the winter's smoke
In a realm of ant hills

53
Single-seater overhead
Drones away the long afternoon
And a stranger's voice
Lost among gorges
Far off along split ridges
—To be honest, a mystery—
Shouts this single warning:
'Hallo lost voyager!'
To a realm sundered
Split peaks eat their planes
And pointilize downed sirens
In grievous bellies

54
She sweeps blue resin from milky sky
Thunderbird, blue-beaked rascal, roving-eyed wanderfiend
Her wings collapse and she plunges away
The high summer noon rings rainless

55
Beaten circles once marked seasons atop the plateau
Now creosote struggles amid the monoliths
And equinoctial suns rise in proper place
Beams meant for ancient eyes are now a milky dissipation

56
Waylaid beetles multi-write
Horace symbols in the sand
Scrape dung paths together
See evidence of the divine

57
One thing to never be called—
'Coward'
Stepped into ragged moonlight
A long racing way ahead

58
Whippoorwill upcanyon
Will o' the wisp
Whatever, if you will
Pass on the fluty secret
From hill-country domain
Chrysanthemum-voiced
Enchanté, santé
Luck
This voice reassuringly mild
Humble miner returns
From an upcountry camp
Lantern on the bodega's point
Shines the magic words into
Still night to hear
Golden darkness here
'All is well
I go about the business now
I, going, arrive,
And going, I arrive
Wherever you will and
So where I fly
Rest, peace, and god-grace
Be with you merry gentlemen'
Santé, salud, cheers

59
Spines stick in the palm
With small sight let them out
Barbs shrink into infinite distance;
The recursive properties of cactus

60
MARTINEZ'S SUMMIT
On top, leaning in to phantom fire,
As bedridden winds toss storm sheets
Like ripped canvas atmospherics
Let loose the high-pitched dynamite sky
Night overthrown,
A fear of trees
Like crashing vampired spines
Cracking on dread
All morning soft rain
Raise the flap and snow
An inch melting quickly
Soddenly
The trailing sheets—
Three sheets to the wind
Have fallen here

61
A brilliant star flies on morning wings
Over country hot and dusted
She burns through webbed retinas
Casts shadows to starry sea

62
The lantern offers beguiling perimeters
Crossed by hydra-headed insects
A chorus of bleating cicadas
Enshrouds wine-deeps of night

63
We made our way down, the cliffs echoing with gravelfalls
And crashed through the undergrowth cutting vines
Then all lay silent and I knelt at creek's edge
Sweat surprisingly tickled the tip of my nose

64
Atop the sun-blasted ridge
Rifle tucked into the shoulder and 500 meters to spare
From ill light comes a beshapen figure
Two then, listless, who float on skirts of the breeze

65
Soaring raincloud-winds breach the peak
In a non-moon time
Embers glimmer, pulse to wilder gusts
Feed a breathy creature in crouched bedrock

66
A point hovers on the cape of the mountain
Flashes a downing S-O-S
This is my star
Fallen to your hand

67
Where I stand
Chrysalis rock
At an hour of night
A phantom leopard strayed
Casting shaded eyes
On hills beyond
Perhaps he's there yet
Or here among the
Clattered earthen bowels
I stake myself
That it's not my turn
That he's been led astray
Or fraught with fear
And looking once, twice
Keeping in the valley sight
Hillocks feign
Bright rubble in the day
By this I set my stride
Goodbye cruel place,
Place to crawl to die
The sun near horizon lies
Time then, away

68
Voices dart from spiny fields
Those of birds in hidden hovels
Laid in legg'ed twisting cactus
Not to be too outspoken or adventurous

69
A layer of thirst
Low plight of the mice
Witchcraft rumors drift thick as
Dust through caked paper hills

70
In the night
Amongst live reeds
And sunbaked sage
A phantom stream slid past,
Once sun had baked it back
It came no more
Sank underground
Stayed sleeping
Resilient, restful
Hibernatory, stranger to the light
Below the crust
What treasures there lurked
What things beautiful to delight
Wait, long day
Please rest, I ask,
For wondrous night-delights

71
Serpent lairs lie
In a tangled labyrinthine mass
Mesquite *bosque* deeps hold
Torn bowers; a redoubt for eels

72
Remember that we are only visitors here
Open secret stores
Sow golden grain and
Shine unto others

73
AUGUST-TIDE
Torrid sunlight
Reflects campanile towers
Rifts of thunderheads
Thundermaking cloud-seeded country
Like drums, cannon fire
Kalashnikov-straddling
Beachcomber craziness
Fritted tittle-tattle
Titillating palisades
Heavy crashing showers
Wood-driving riptide
All-ensconcing washingness
Nothing wise
All young, Augustinian
Early age of lightning
Outside in pants, no shirt
Power-outing weather
Full-power curtailing
Wind, rain, hail
Zeus somewhere laughing
And laying the world to waste

74
Relishing pants off
I cry aloud to thunderheads
It's warm time
Summer sinking to fall
Bees under bottlecaps
Rattling home
And the sly lizard winks
Withdraws to cracked rocks
So sharp is the sun
In indolent air, at the
Shimmering hunting spot

75
Hot like Hell, or as Hell was
Is it summertime
There too?
Because here we have
Cicadas threatening the trees
And hammering pulsing notes
Candles melt for lack of fire
Disinclining themselves
Plastic awnings secretly implode
The buzz under the steps
Yes is a rattlesnake
Go the other way
My heart like a rusted oil dragon
Beats lumbering cadence
Beer with my pants off
In the shade of the tamarisk out back
Dust from a tractor hangs still
A fan like sleeping underwater
Washes me in the long evening
The birds have left
The neighbors have left
I'm still sitting here

76
Place the shotgun
Against the bark and slumber
There'll be no rabbits
Here waiting

77
Until only the mountain remembered
The birds drafted from the currents
Bent creatures finished pacing
The lofty mount remained

78
One day I emerge gauntly victorious
Vivified, salutorious
From a secret upcountry reach
Tramping down on unsteady boots blooded
Ripped pants, *pistola*
Sweat-braided brim
Thumbs at the seams
Button-bare and thread-tied gusto
Like a man on fire I reach the high road
Enter life with people fattened
Ordinary garbage time
No one welcomes me or stops, stares in anguish
At a free man poor
So then
Glancing back at ways I've come
Nothing out of place
All right

79
Ledge rocks split with offerings of
Well-thumbed dust implements
Burnt, scorched semi-godly wild structures
Cthulu time, lost underworld spot
Locked in rock on rock on rock
Seeking issuance ungodly
Right demon-just root-times
Before Christianity
No loinclothed Christ to stop
An infested wilderness seething
Stoppered, wet with bleeding
Ants carry knowledge
Of pre-time

80
Sonorous mountain bell
Brassly
Rings movements of
Far-off livid war

81
Spare oaken hollow
Old California
Dusk beyond dusky
Wooden lamplight
Crotchety limb
Places placeless
Firesworn dimly
Branches go
Grow into coal-face
Yip yipee-oo
Ferns stray
Lamplit beyond
Circle of warmth held dearly
Closely, never-let-go-ly
Around, within, beyond
Airy nettled silence settles
Coils upon high reaches
Netherspace
Breath of wool curls
Shorn smoke winders
Autumnal creeping
Ill-light
Dark-light
Nether-to-light ho

82
HOUSE OF THE MUSHROOM
Limbered beings
Walk the heights free
Forgotten arenas
Welcome non-church places
Sun worshippers
Mushroom houses
Unwieldy bark
Cleft nails in soft wood
Mountain hollows
Candle-lit rockface
Draped in rich garlands
No cuneiform script, written things
Just burnt offerings
Scorched clarity
Sonorous bell
Early times and spring shine

83
AN INHERITANCE OF ANTS
What about time with
Radial centers?
Before humankind walked,
What then?
No subconscious direction
Nor points like ants
Marked the way?
Colored lizards crisscrossed the stone's face
And they, not we, were fated

84
With continuously
Less-pulverized eyes
Sight the peak
Now in hailing distance

85
With rhythmic breaths
Grasp each ledge
Rise above
The unconquerable summit

86
The harpsichord thicket hides
Rib-cage branches
Carry on
Under signs of serpents

87
Just a trickle yet
And, knee-taken, we drink
Gelatin drops cling to our eyebrows
An upcanyon bird shrieks

88
I woke this morning
With a belly full of memory
Had I swallowed them last night?
Where had I gone?

89
NOVEMBER
In November sometime
Death belongs
Fit not where, just how
In winding silent land
Stray not at dusk
Stay not through silent *nacht*
Wellspring of the deep

90
STEAKS
With blackened branch
Turn the *papas*
In their charred creased wrapping
Roll them out of the
Smoking embers
Cheery little spirits laugh
Now slide the grill
Now the steaks
Nicely softened
Press them carefully
Between black tongs
The beer bottle glistens
Behind the hand
Right where it should be

91
Rock-on-rock clatter from the hilltop
It again!
I peer up
Nowhere does it emerge

92
Ghosts emerge in the
Upcanyon nightfall
Car is far away
I feel in the darkness

93
Eerie land
That did deign to face the day
Open your innards to me
Secret long-winding ways
Unearth sand runnings
With woodsmoke low
Land like early times
Undeciphered
Wood spirits gather
Halloo morphological
Layered, tiered wild

94
The little spider descends
He has some guts
Approaching me
He climbs back up

95
When the moon ups
Night denizens howl news
With crescent light
The hunt is on

96
She circles far in arcing light drowning
Glorious pathos
Paths below—
Trails far and leading
None lies true but all go arcing
This region twisted
Lies fallow from prying
The secret's safe
That doves and mice go mourning
Arrow-wed wilderness
Land of loss and blossoms
Red pearlish ocotillo
Yes—the answer waiting
So long to come
Yes she says to weary care
Yes to winging high
Yes

97
Heartache and briers
Over there she cries
Like a lost child I once tried to call her
Perhaps a he
No importa porque es coyote
Denizen of the flat
Royal wanderer of the canyons
She cries, he cries
Along fated river's bend

98
Hail cracks in dawn
Black window veins and absolute sky
Arise my friends
It's twig-witching time

99
The coyotes hunt
With guttural voices
Scrape hard-packed earth
Feed on gizzard, gibbet, feet and tongue
Chew through matted hair
They wail in winding desolation
Far below, dreaming
I now hear this chorus
Risen to widened moonrise
I listen as the door hangs open
As they hurry, crowd, catch
Amidst hectic cries, a
Wrestled feeding time

100
COYOTE BY THE RIVER
Across the river there below
He calls with gentle cries
The girl he lost
And goes
No effort needed
About his wander-way
Past Meander's stream
Seeks a spot for washing memory
In two months' time
This course will dry
He'll pick up the seeking way
Tonight he carries cries
Above beauty's
Pallid night
Like water bearers' sighs

101

DIRECTIONS FOR MAKING HOT CHOCOLATE

The gift and trick
To making hot chocolate
Is a small sharp fire
High stars
And one tin cup
Place the cup in the
Bloom of flames with
The water
And let the steam come
To billow
Like volcanic ashes
Then take one packet
Hot chocolate (brand unimportant)
Stir the powder to a froth—
That's good
Stir with a stick
And if there's little water
In your pack
It makes the cup taste sweeter
Gently dip and
Purr and lift
Then cool it with cupped hands
And sip
There!
Now is that better?

102

He lay quietly to one side and passed
Knowing finally his careful place to rest
Between two stones, one small, one large
The pup grew long-sighted
Ceased his breath
Lay still with small paws crossed

103
Upon the ledge at the end of the valley
Where devils meet in fall and blooms in spring
A wild pup counts her sodden breaths
Organs suck at water and she faints
The pack has left for it's a starving year
To her the countryside rings white
And fills with sounds of water

104
Perched at the very edge
Clung a lone juniper
Which had dried
In an unmemorable summer
And gave up the ghost
Yet remained pinned
At boulder's edge
Tight at commanding point
She kept her feet for
Three or four years more
Fooling no one
Against the sky
With brittle branches
Her fluid trunk a 'J'
She held two sparrows' nests
With one branch
Missing
Converted into woodsmoke

105
Wooded drape'd slopes
Hear my cry
Like a wheeled arrow
Tossed between clouds

106
Hohoba sprig swells, glistens
Languorously pulses
Amid flames brash
The lowcountry wafts woodsmoke

107
Content like a cave-dwelling moth
Sharing place with pack rats
I sit, self-surrounded
With bitter dry branches

108
With a blackened roof lip
The fork'ed cave angles
Over nested pit
What was starry-roasted here?

109
Wide awake, the cub
Finds a new form of looking
Rise, little one
Watch these silent hills

110
For thousands of suns
Slow-passing rains
Buried the mossed rock
Amongst fringed willows

111
Evergreen wisps
Descend abrupt cliffs
Late light perches atop
The sunstruck crevasse

112
Little cactus callers clap on to barrels
Sound notes of throbbing
Clapboard calling
Stickled homes in heated weather

113
Dearth settles
Over land of mice and rabbit holes
Weather-fretted changes
Caused the oaks to die
Giving homes no longer
Deer have traipsed elsewhere
The snow has come early
To blasted wooden hides
And dry, scaled bark
Hard of hearing
Falls to forage bitter ground
Calls no names in spellbound thinness
Seedpot husks rot
Tapered trunks lose
Their upright posture
Bristlecones peel to sand

114
The curling paper plate
Dies like a seething amulet
Embers jolly and suck it in
It heads skyward, shredding

115
The cool moon slides away
And a griffin dawn thunders,
Cannon fodder clouds
Shred and lose grey way

116
It's an accidental rain tonight
It stops for a breather
Hurries on

117
The branch with a soul of a snake
Pauses in the way
Too late to turn, I leap
Better to be safe than sorry

118
Harried *cuervos* in the air
Seek ebb'ed solace
Find brick-dry bones and snake lairs nigh
In hunger-fettered land

119
It is a low surreal eve
Lamplight pierces the thicket
Moth wings dampen
Tepid-born time
Drowsy hillocks slumber in
Advancing, scintillating dew

120
An orange lantern rises
From clouds of shredded foam
Beyond my flickering beam
Rabbits dive in brush

121
He, slinking down, reading
Rests an eye on
The smoldering campsite
Tail follows into reeds

122
I am a student of the skies
Through dawn, noon, eve
And night
Follower of wilted tracks
Tepid mark'ed plottings
Seeker having sought
Waters, streambeds, gullyways
Breathe, tread, and feel as the blind
Then return to glimpse again

123
Wind breaks on the ridgeline
Like voluptuous coils of water
It rips deaf barrier
This all-charging torrent

124
Voices in the gale
Strike the mountaintop winter
A garrulous pitched battle
Wilderness haunting-time

125
Craft-shorn amber tree
Serpent skin peels by the
Destitute hag pillar
Wild fallen crow home

126
The stream has passed its yearly mark
And now munches at the cliff
Cuts and shoots black water under
Sturdy walls of pressed debris
Roots like molten marble
Drag rocks to scrub them clean
And rub them raw
Then first one section
Another then and halfway home
The mighty wall
Slips down to torrid current

127
Bladed hillside
Crickets wink in and out
In brush
Such paltry wing'ed stirrings

128
Amongst birds and rushes
Like sweeping broom-ends
A thicket lies
Topped with crystal eve
Dares a silence
'Make a move' it whispers
Simple intentions lie

129
Wizened yearly brush-offs
Old clans stir
Beckon to one another
Across burdened gulfs
Emboldened carnate carnivores
Enmold territory
Stride together, clash ringing
Trade mates, holy places, secret spots
Out-piss one another, then
Yawning, slink away

130
Skies are torn asunder
And a startled rain comes
A thousand rolling beetles
Clamor in torn seed beds

131
GARGOYLE FALCONS
And then they came
Out from highland grottoes
At some undetermined point
Wakened, sped then down and near
Came within hailing distance
And sent the spine tingling
With ribald fretful drabble
Like loose arrows
Calling out demons
Awakened drastic things through night unlimited
Cascading calls issued waking dead
Yawing wide-mouthed eager
Overlaid teeth and best-laid plans
Like gargoyle falcons resting upon one hilltop
Then another they came
Too numerous
Too beyond, too escaped
At one with forces unseen, unknown, disowned
Not here but came from
Someplace else
The ranges ringing with their voices
Jungle chants
Tattered ambiguous dexterity

132
Inhabit borders of the earth
Warm beds of coal
Time rubs against itself
Stunted trees once were florid

133
Starry-roosted night
That dimly through you
Can be seen high heavens
Stars quieten as
A ship of the air
Brightly-lit against eternity
Lazes into line
And smokes a path
Thin, true, obliviously
Travels slightly by

134
Coffee-dark curds stain the mug
And I wipe my thumbs
Along the seams of my pants
Stand, shake the day on

135
Shelter with beaten hands
The howling stove
Breathe sour flames
Rock on flaked boot heels

136
One more log
Must steadily decay
To glowing moldings
Then I'll bid ring'ed sky goodnight

137
Steam wafts from the boiling pot
I wash my face
Rub my eyelids
And lave my arms goodnight

138
Gargantuan megalithic causeway
Checkerboard sky
Here's a tumbled jackknife ridge
Humus-jostled tide-form

139
Gorge waters sound the
Turbid fight
Resounding pit-fallen foam
Descends the crystal causeway

140
CABRILLO CANYON
That people passed here is certain
In the hot time
Ragged jeans lie bunched
Knotted with sweat
And boots laceless sit beside the way
They hurried quickly and serenely
Plastic bottles were crushed
Hecho en Mexico
Jugo de fresa
By boulder's fire ring
One stage, one sitting-spot
Towards going the long way

141
COMPATRIOTA
Ay, *compadre*
I know your special kind of humor
To cross the mountains in summer
Ay, *compatriota*
You top it off and
Bring it to your lips once more
Before the real work begins
Si, *compatriota*
If they find you they will turn you away
If the desert finds you she slays
Better not be found
Ay, *compatriota*
Sing your *norteño canciones*
But quietly
For you're crossing tonight
Ay, *compatriota*
Leave him against the stone
If he cannot walk he cannot drink
Ay, *compatriota*
They tell me you're a risk
But you risk everything
Ay, *compatriota*
Lay you down in shaded orchards
Slick with mud
Ay, *compatriota*
Rest in the fields
Like a hare ready to run
Compatriota
What if one man has something
And the other nothing?
What do you do if no one mourns?
And morning doesn't come?

142
What compels imagination
Lies beyond the firelight
Arced with night
Go out and settle the vision

143
In the reeds and rushes the head lies still
With body looped away like a spotted tube
She meditates
Wakes softly
Her viper's tongue flicks the air
She feels a tremble
From a footfall
Far distant

144
The cicadas in the eucalyptus
Pulse with energy
I lie, heat-enervated
Pop another crisp beer

145
Smoketree—smoke bush
Droning grey bees harvest her
And trim silken branches
With roots placed resolutely
She holds still for balance
In the soft ripe air

146
Lone abrupt timber post
Holds mesa-sway
Bides falling night goodnight
Ember rain whips grasses

147
The tent flap sways
In the early morning cold
El dia ha llegado
Around the vacant fireplace

148
The lizard cannot be seen
He thinks, can he?
But there he rests
Bobble-headed guardian

149
Scraped coals brush together
Rise in flames
Send whooshing warmth through brush
Quail sing for silence

150
Origin-curve of washbed
Creeping wildflower friends
Cluster, send on
The fallen *palo verde*

151
He passed, stopped, backed
Curious, came to the foot of the blaze
Long-tailed tremulous wonder
The hungry kangaroo rat

152
With arcing light like a welder's torch
The sun emerges from shelving peaks
Cleft rocks spit steam
The crofts are alive
Flies drop, grass shrivels
Stunning heat's a frightful wonder
Disperses the living
Phoebus' chariot descends
Burns out eyes of tender leaves
Smokes purple flowers' retinas
It skins with raw atomic power
An age has ended
Hell sweeps low
Snuffs out the scarce survivors

153
The marshland sinks underfoot in
This haunted ancestral hall
Arrowweed *tuileries*
Are anxious onlookers
This faintest deathly stir of wind
Means the cliff is near
Wend a faint way
Knife in hand for sawing
Through trilled boonies

154
A built hut, *castillo*
On stalwart point
Gazes far to fallow country
Peaked bowl of tiered passes

155
This one stone
Has the intricate maze-work
Pave'd lengthened paths
And crusted skin to stop my way
I was going somewhere now forgotten
Place it atop the low overhang
Marking to return

156
Past parched groves
Splintered wood, decrepit gullies
Pale earth falls away
And freshened night lauds the land

157
Ring around the moon
Predatory ancients squelch her
She cries unheard
And makes a wish to glow

158
Eggs, bacon, ham, toast
Roast coffee, hot mug
Dim bulb
Breakfast before entering the unknown

159
Cut a charcoal mark
Where the ridgeline lies
Streak it underfoot
Cream paper shows the work

160
Beat fresh arms and face
Warm muscles tauten to the tread
Blue country
Cold morning trailhead

161
One piece'd stone
Like an ancient jewel set
In carbuncled clay
Balances the cliff

162
Atop the great dune
Overlooking valley wide
A lonesome mortared fireplace
Awaits human warmth

163
Ambivalent wing'ed children
Twirl gyrations atmospheric
The cliff rooks shed scat and shell
Colored stones and bits of straw
Drop into the void beyond
Anguished mothers' cries

164
Shattered trees, old trail, a
Pockmarked truck's hood
Falcons nest in thistles
Parse spiny new world wonders

165
The long shape slides away
And the small firelit circle
Shrinks, colder
A canyon rim sighting

166
Leap rock to rock
Down the narrow streambed
Hum happily along
No toe testing the way

167
THE UNKNOWN VISITOR
In twisted agave narrows
And a black boulder field
An abandoned trail
Turns in to rest under
Unknown morphological signs of
Hunters, bows and whistles
Nameless things that watch
Lie shrouded and still
Uncalled names
Dark shamans rise from pitched earth
No one passes in day
Nor eventide
Amongst the fetid bracken
A silent table
Crevassed puddle
Silent valley
A deathsong hilltop
Peak'ed fear-watch
Reeking baked rocks
Empty daylight spent
In revolving round hollows
Night circles emerge
Throb against the horizon
The encroaching dwarvish forest
Whistles a spitting tune
Skin drums beat in the boulder field
Pulverized rock sifts
Dust to the trail

168
Huddle in the sleeping bag
Pellets of wind
Claw thin tent fabric
A night for midnight snow dancing

169
PROCESSIONAL
Arms eager to embrace
Float through declining trails
The scratchiness and sandy bottom
Holds you, my love
I am above somewhere calling
For you to come home
A long journey is completed
There is nothing left
But bread crumbs in the cupboard
We eat, hands taken together
What was dry roasted here
Was lost and then found
All the open trailings wave us forward
Our family of humanity beckons across the sandy grain
No longer completely alone
Now
I wait for you to open your eyes
A child
Open your eyes, *mi nena*
Through lean tidings
While salty breeze and roiling mist
Rises slowly across the world
Wipe the sweat away
Take bites from candlelight
Stolen hours
This is your hour, girl, such an hour!
Cutting blundered dark to squares of cloth
We carve up worldly blackness
The land has wasted away
It has weakened on limbs of tarnished silver
Let me lift you from the table, from the tableland
Open your eyes, my love
Somewhere a twanging guitar string
Plucks first notes

170
What figures
This old ocotillo has seen?
He rests, leaning
Looks away for a spell

171
Something, I couldn't see it
Rested here a pause ago
Leaned in mournful pose
As I trod the sandy bottom

172
And then it melted
Unbeknownst while sleeping
Shifting in the bag
The ice slid away

173
In river's heart the rocks toss
Splinter, roll, clash
Night-becalmed air
Carries a symphony of rattle

174
Thunder pools and
Stale air seethes at the boundary
In high wastes
A fresh breath stirs

175
Whipping night wind
Tosses fire sparks low
Downcanyon gusts
Lose lights to the void

176
In a *mescla* of
Peeled rocks
Lie innards of the wash
Somewhere underneath
Broad ways in soil
Reaches disinterred
Fallow land lies looped
Sways bent earth
Untoward grizzled peaks
Contrary grace
Within-beneath-almost
Squeezed, shot, upended
Unfilled, upturned
Jagged debris field
Broad wash sunk asunder
Hardscrabble home
Lyrical disjointed dishwash field of years
Greatland hard path
The long reach ends
The wash upfills
Cuts cake-rock
Dribbled layers rise
To be picked through
By crows
Careful wanderers

177
Crack fresh eggs in the pan
Wet morning
Birds and *palo verdes*
Shrug off dew falls

178
Glowing cigar—night cool
Cherubic end drips fire
Smooth smoke
Gusto-puffing

179
On the land
Fear fades
Unbends stomach pangs
A desire for safe passage

180
In high-grown fields and
Rock-bitten bights
Find silver sleep
With northern stars as company

181
Water bubbles song and
Crickets play their dusky calls
In low-ceilinged evening
Onset of amber summer

182
HALLOWEEN
Strange calls float on Hallow's Eve
Frangipani lights
And lust-orange Jupiter
Cross the silken glowworm sky

183
Light sky
Dark land
Night of the full moon
Dias perdidos
Ruta del tortuga
They lose the tortured way
Drink from chipped glass
Sleep under torn sheets
Stoop to carry the burden
Follow paths to freedom
They pause in arroyos
Start out of fear
Stop when overcome
Make their way
One step at a time
Entre realidad y sueño
Light land
Dark sky
Day of the partial sun

184
Although the *Olla podrida* bakes
Nearby sings a quail covey
Ring'ed familiars
Witches' bush coven

185
With earthen voices
Spirits chant in high country
Currents wash jasper
A cavern, empty, faces rolling gorge

186
Star-cloaked swollen land
Spire pregnant
Cools thatched
Driftwood peaks

187
Like an inverted river
Smoke streams downcanyon
Twirls, dissipates
In somnolent lost air

188
The tibial stench hangs low
Over soil rich with flies
A dried blood-bake
Death in the outcrop

189
Charcoal fox ears
Mask of twilight
Thunderclaps count
Between earth and sky

190
UP TO THE SPIRE
The lost battlement spire
Snags ocean's twilight
Eternal lense
Tall wandering minstrel
Rock-groomed clover
Eggshell spittle, wind grass
Spare death above
Slender bedrock rivulets
Crusted amulets
Sheerface russet overhangs
A charged windward trail leads
Past broken bits upward
To shocked facetower

191
Ancient fallen bookcase
Scattered tomes, great works
Parched pages
Crumpled trees and books are similar

192
A spun dissolute star sets
The far point plummets, a
Pinwheel lustered low-ceilinged orb
Imperceptibly glitters in the gathering dark
The creas'ed upper orbit-forge
Sweeps down this star in season
Hot light on the horizon

193
With hollow-leg'ged gait
Stroll an endless persimmon mile
With Abyssinic lion jitters
Walk off season-tide hunger

194
In the crackling far forest
Shadowed forms spin
Lose the long sun
Spirit-flecks flash in lowering light

195
The storm blows ash
Grasses shred in passing
Watered winds fly
Press nettles, fickle brambles

196
Under disassembled sky
A lute-sounding emptiness
Flurry-blown wilds
Strike a grey-lorn note

197
In utter silence a flurry settles
Through whirling east wind
A smoketree sparks against cream sky
Fog descends again

198
He arises, age'd hare
Sidles off
Leg-down on steaming sand, the
Deliberate siesta over

199
A dark cloud-pause falls
Wipes stellar transience away
White rifts
Pour in the sheeted backland

200
As if the undulating form
There in the thistle
Knew the mouse
Had fled

201
Sure that the trail
Is a new way
I pause wearily
Sighting the fence post

202
Across the Americas
Mountains quake with happy will
Shiver along marbled spines
Alma-yerbas de tierra natal

203
Unsettled voices strike
Clear notes from eve
Creatures soft-spoken
Sink with the wind

204
Hole tone
Settles low
In brackish country
Note of the wind cave

205
Hunger pangs set themselves
Within diluted eyes
Sitting, yearn to stand
Standing, hope to rest

206
The red hawk's
Dalliance at the churn
Sets off
Explosions of protest birds

207
In the sprung canyon hollow
Tireless beetles
Carve gravel banks
October is death-dry

208
Whiskey shot by firelight
Chilly amber mist
Red-stirred mash
Sharp like rainwater

209
Intrepid traveller
Dallies in hill country
Forlorn streams
Feed his route

210
Nothing so filling
As a good burp
After steak and mashed potatoes
Vinegar swirls in the plate

211
Curveting snow
Wraps the campsite in
A pallid spell of biers
No one waits

212
From this jagged, blasted core
Of the gnarled trunk
One last limb
Reaches skyward

213
Then the owl returned
Focused in the darkness
'Here', he said
'I see you, I see you'

214
Come, screeching
Jittery nonanimal embers
Grey fuzzy wuzzy soul-capturers
Redefine true north
True lust and hunger
Come near and set wits
To lowly something
Finding its lone way
Lost bedeviled simpleton
Such as many more
Mysteries exhale breath and
Thus are sought
Seeking, find this outer wailing
Out of time and deeps comes form
Out of form come things beyond

215
Grey lizard coils to the stone
His white tail glows
The other lost
In a rare scuffle

216
Out of brackish silence
A featherweight word declaims
Still your heart and listen
For vernacular tongues apace grim ledges

217
In the stillborn paternoster thicket
Slow-silted herbs
Have woven wicker nets
The herded wind whips round and round

218
Tilted rock at high noon
Lone buzzard carves torrid circles
Her shadow a grey passing
The peak leaches russet

219
Birds call up the silty bend
The bedrock pool has warm stripes
Tadpoles, evaporation rings
Bees frolic in algaeic melody

220
Like a family of biblical Jews
They, flustered, flutter
Trail, coalesce, pick and chime
Quail find seeds wherever they go

221
Meditations on the nightfall
Unsung hero stratosphere
Ill-brought bow'ed glowingness
Somewhere fine wave'd flight
Shirks falling fright
Last, least, lost
Thoughts above below are tossed
Let air fall
And upon the gloaming
Haunting ever-fizzling dreamtime
Let glimpses sail
Flecks rain, let down—
Something above shifts
Patterned light so merely weightless
So weightless, such lackluster
Delightfuling never-endedness
Firm underlying soil like a
Stage by which all plays
And clocks and hearts are set
Let these wassailing travails
Cry foul and slice such sky
The earth lets up, holds
Lets the remembering by

222
Filleted longbow branch
Thick as meat
Branch I said
That one resting momentarily
Between glowing and passing up
In sparks and molded embers
Such cradle of passageways and things solitary
This spark goes out to all the mites
About to lose a home

223
Fresh juniper lies knotted closely
No hawks *ni aguilas pasan*
Grass is like knife blades in the
Dwarf forest of the north face

224
Backboned ridge leads solely upwards
There, fountless, becragged, rests an
Electric oceanic vista
Jeweled granite meets wanderlust mice

225
SITE OF THE KILL
Discover a welter of *huellas mezcladas*
Inhuman prints and signatory mathematics
Cyclic prances sprawled into one another, a
Dance of earthly death and astronomic numbers, of
Forefeet and panicked twistings
The bloodened pursuit that ended so dearly
Tuft of fur, the arching corpse devoured

226
This ancient country is
Land without king
God alone is borne by mesa gardens
Burnt ridgelines

227
Shattered peaks harbor
Elephantine crags to soak in russet sun
Wind *djin* beings
Stand at the tide of night

228
It was just a trunk
Stout, made of fine leather
I carried it to camp
In dying light
Its fingers dragged at the sand and I didn't light it
The undulating arms were too comely
The busty wooden brassier pitiful
It lay on its side unbroken beside the tent
Overcome with sorrow
Where it scratched at night
Slept throughout the day

229
Emerging from the backcountry
Smell beef on the wind
Straight from the boiling pot
Chainsaws mill on a steel-blue afternoon

230
Late summer
Crickets fade
It's not too late to plant pumpkin
Spider webbings lie dormant

231
In hollow's deeps bees play
Last sun's rays stretch low and
Night's shadow falls to sand
Smooth stone radiates reticent day

232
Evocative rising dust, yonder hills
By what scrubbing rose the *polvo*?
Slip through mottled leaves, sun-spotted
A named human seeks otherworldliness
Day patterns
Overarching greatness stretches to contain
Floating spirit and inhabitant of nether-planes
Yonder mite goes about on tractor business
Dry blown grass, seeded plateau

233
Open land, and the knock of the cloud formation breaks
If sitting we see stillness and by stillness see movement
So every wild stroke of brush lifts its thatch head
Ants stream their paths and globules wet the shining earth

234
A latticework of trails tied far lands up in generous knots
Gaps in the rock sent hunters and wedding parties on
Drilled shells and handiwork scattered, and bits of twine blew
When cloak'd muleteers came from southern shores with gifts

235
Scattened, overflown finger grasses hail
Diseased outcroppings
Brother-well-met
Forests of the plain

236
FEBRUARY
Along the near slopes
While February drives
Such drizzles turn fickle
Rain tops snow
Thus raining, paving
Strikes cleft rocks open
To dry the humidity of a hundred years
The chants of
Hardy deadly dry-living wash spirits
Come through and rise
Relive sweet remembered springs and parchment days
Let not fickle perils perish
Nor sands whiten
Yes February, pallid pall-bearer
Carries broken branches near
Closes the way
Locks a new time
Strikes a hollow stone
And grizzled haunted washes
Ring with sounds of thunder
A dozen pourings
Freshen tails for bush-maidens

237
Drops crenellate the window pane
Mist packs low hills
And scenes of desperate cold sink further
Tonight's no time for outing
Wisdom rests in places, watches distant
Burnished battlemounts submerge in frothy waves
The cold travels ancient walls
Pries with stunted fingers austropithic ledges
Sings cyanic dirges
And winter rises again
Cold flame of blizzard
Faces in mountain deeps
The unraveled jacket by the door drips frigidity

238
Crenellated apiaries buzz out
Wings studded, befreckled, glitter
Dance of the jeweled honeycomb
Glazed antechambers wilt

239
Coffers of heaven shock the hurtled sky
The cavernous abyss
In a peace of dawn-drowned hills
Reverberates rubble

240
From demon's cavern beneath the peak
Flit forth peak'ed creatures
To mock, transmute the scene
Libyanic beetling swarm

241
PART ONE
The plants, alive
Unfettered hill sprites
Drowsy reed boys
Grassy girls long-plaited
Sky-watching sylvan ones

PART TWO
Stones alive
Hard-edged granite clusters
Surly stone-cutters
Fluted, varnished peers
Ridge-perched rollickers

242
Drops land in confusion
Split the flames
Like children's hands seeking knees
A columnar gyre pours forth

243
The gift of heat *se enfria*
As from a city with high windows
Lies a glowing reach grown ancient
Dies in dust

244
Shellacked griffin peak
Limelight wanes
Frozen blue shard
Unworded sky-castle
Dipping night rook
Flick'ring wings
Crusaders, flight of aileroned whippets
And the hour strikes
Tangled abundance
Masses shunt from lost crevasses, the
Air thick with legs
Sky channels open
Rivulets multidimensional
A horde traffics forth

245
House of the mushroom, host of wilderness
Dreamt-of dawn spreads far to yellow boulderites
Birds sing over vapor lenses
Fire-blackened rock

246
Thus saith the crow
Going to his house
'Caw, call again'
He's out
Gone hiding or hunting
Lonesome being
Breathe his name once in the wilds
He, perching, listens

247
Jagged bluffs
Torn backside, bloody palms
Wet prints of the passage
Mark the cherry rock for life

248
Yucca trail lost in the mind-hearing
Lost in the seeing, in the feeling
Damp roots and muddy rains churn
Outside of eons gilt with native light
Mark time like the sandaled canyon runner
Crush the seeds
Drink cactus milk with bloodened fingers
Mash arrow spines and sprouting flowers
Glaze the eyes with honeysuckle beads
Still the heart bleating like a lamb in season
Remember the guarded wells
Pots in slim defiles held against sandy season
Brilliant legs follow hands
As they brush yucca needles
A passive wanderer travels in
Diffusing spring

249
Fetching bounty with raw boots
The lone gatherer rises
Crushes lavender between her fingers
Breathes the gathering storm

250
Rock ducks on the lonely path
A gust of wind
Lantern-poppies
Branches scratch the breathing way

251
Walk ledges of cairn-formed dolomite
Egyptian eye, soaring Eastern star
Violet penumbral plain
Smoke of the smoketree, hallowed eve

252
Like oligarchs
Enjoying sunset mornings
Through mountainous caverns
The wide-bellied behemoths
Stride across landwastes
They pace
Skin shelving
Encrusting into
Commoners, vista beholders
Like-minded on-high praising
Loafers, world shaper-watchers
Travellers nigh
Forlorn glory groupies
Glassed in by sky
Low might
Sudden flight of fancy
It is true what they say
That every mountain
Monster crumbles to the sea?
Not one remains
Untoppled, unfallen lies?

253
Guests' faces are lit against ribbons of night
Ghosts come in force to knock fire sparks away
And in the blank black, friendly creatures, soundless, sleep
Guardians of winter tales

254
Rabbit lairs twist in furrows
Past peeled juniper palings
Veined grasshopper wings
Molder in rich earth

255
I wait for sweet wet song
Ravens sprinkle straw at blackened day
And boarded clouds shear away
Fill no basins deep nor long

256
It howled all night
And in the dawn, dark against the sky
Stood sleek storm clouds
Shifting sheets of grey

257
Stork-trees
Colorless winter twist-dancers
Long limbs lance white dawn's tide
Fly from a howl-land grove

258

CAST INTO THE GALE

Into the night, then, with ear-shot crashing
Trees uprooted fell
Hammered loose soil and
Splayed themselves in veil-like snow
Thundered like a horde of winter-beasts
Berserk in cradle-dark
A ripping of tent-flaps
Stones the size of heads glanced
Into the bottomless anvil gale
Pulse-sparked wind shot a hail of gravel
Into spitting formless night
Uplift-winds surged and split trunks
Eyes without pupils stirred pure wrath
Distant lightning danced
Skull of the sheep god and boulder giant
Weather the glorious storm on the great mountain

259

Like ordered columns marching away, away
Lovely stones stride along
In rain, polished dusk, mountain-sweats of August, November, July
Away
A throbbing beat amongst the hills
Passes alone, away
A smoke signal
Hapless watcher
Shining plain
Plain August noon
Marching on and away

260
Under heathen pine and ribbonwood
Fresh snow-spirits stalk
Ice storms shift down
Hear guttural moans from the mountain

261
Wood-serenaded breach
Rockland passage
A tying together of many times
Kudzu gulch *déjà vu*

262
As *luna* set, the glint of
A thousand points
Streamed from packed beds
To reflect a vacuous *cielo*

263
Yellow feelers of heaven
Have painted the brush gold
A yawing chasm opens to the
Soaring eye-of-the-sky

264
Stunted oaks soak the damp
Welcome little scurriers underfoot
Sniff moisture from rattled soil
Ebb-tide of the cut moon

265
The leaves so early picked
By Beethovenic wings
Depart from windy clutches
Lay life's crumple 'cross the land

266
ASLEEP IN THE PALMS
Wake with noxious overtones of a hinterland dream
A lantern star sails in
High sky overhead
Fronds beat rushes yet
So curl deep down
Descend and drift
Seek back to whence it came
In apoplexy lies a maze
Trample sodden moors of star color

267
I awoke with eyes gleaming
Heard the tide of autumn shifting
With soft hissing breeze
A starry fall of night

268
Mountain fortresses in the dim wet
Fodder of smoky cloud
Crenellated ridges and portcullis arches
Ocotillos march on crumbled walls

269
Moon an eye of the deep
Clouds like scudding
Of an overturned ocean
Depthless prism of waters

270
Along rocky biers
And untrammeled lense of sky
He made his solitary way
With chest aching to heaven

271
Mesquite smoke upcanyon
Heathen scents brush the breeze
This fire
Cut from a pallor of moth time

272
Ghostheads in the columnar smoke
Moon's eye warps a
A new way of seeing
Smokebath to the pendular stars

273
In the trunk's moonlit shadow
A great silence, crickets beneath branches
Solitary vigil
An embrace of greatness

274
Keep vigil
Under the spreading tree
Grateful to its greatness
Let the legs numb

275
No matter how I walk
I find one rock
Put it in the bag
A new totem

276
RABBIT
You, secret sly one
Are a denizen
Mountebank ilk
Long-shanked
Carpet-eared
You flee as if for no reason
Break brush like fire
Up gully, down canyon
Lilting cry-monger
Impossible speed is a fact
You, fleet-footed bush being
Are impossible
An indescribable rusher

277
As the sun shines through
Animals go out and lick wet rock
Aspirate the sheen
Down cracked gullets

278
Long-hooded warrior
Monstrous sight
Stalking the badlands
Kokopelli jittery hands

279
Crouching, I think something died here
I smell it
Follow the scent
It's my ass

280
Forest of dead ocotillo
Fluctuations on the face of things
Bush-crickets
A parceling out of cloud bursts

281
Cautiously, this silent traveller
Weaves a way through ocotillo
An abrupt bounding of the jackrabbit
Neither assures the other

282
Gather beaded maize
On florid flatlands
Our economy of movement
More ancient than words

283
What is it this wilderness?
Is it sand and bone?
Or ugly dewish bodies
Cut from muck and rock
Intricacy unsurmised
Long-lived stony rambles?
Or rather what are we
That call it something new
When we it never knew?

284
Crows cluck together in
A filial fight
Serious stuff, this banter
Tauntations on fluid air

285
Mottled water
Bits of brine
Birds flit by grassy edge
And a swift sky tarries overhead

286
Withered stalks of century plants
Faros ambientales
In the rose-cheeked sunset
Crash breakers of clouds

287
Find a single piece of pottery
By the trickling wash bed
A dense-hooded rabbit lord
Hides in tarantula warrens

288
Candlestick-orb
Framed by milky clouds
So high, she beckons
'Kiss me now, here'

289
A swirl of thunder
Creosote on the air
A lash of drops
The brash storm sweeps downcanyon

290
Alone at the campsite
A slip of rocks sounds the night
I fire into darkness
Let's find each other differently

291
While those of us
Do not watch
The place grows quiet
A bird flits apace the sky
Fibrous drops
Skin the breath of air
Cut the ashes' skein
Fill the lizards' dens
Revamp said land
Repaint, repair
Replace broken parts
Wash in cascades of mist
Then it's dry time
And the paint thickens
Enmolds, stills, calms, besticks
They thought we saw
With our eyes
But it is only chemistry
Not the vision of the thing
The blind man picked up the
Hammer and saw
I see!

292
Cross-grained guitar strokes
Light of the ascendant half moon
Fire of the heart
Let burn the tangled blood in our veins
Colliding *cellulos*, the heat of laughter
Red love rises to apparating starlight

293
Encilia, wavy breeze, onrushing sky
Set stars, set course, set down, die
Let none take this
None take and eat, swallowing whole
This innate sanctified utter just mystery
I set my stride
Body place I across the way
There is no 'back up' there
The inner escape is here
The year's days flash green
Hills pile a million sufferings
Set myself here, or there
And place the fight
Among these hills remembered

294
Twirled southern skies
Hollows of light
This dryad region
Lets drift a flatland cool

295
Hunted animals avoid night lights
We must go
Deeper and deeper to respire free airs
Deeper into the backcountry

296

Gerfalcon—what is?
Now delirious
Ninety eight and the temp has risen
Much worse and this shall not be fun
Building this
An invisible house
Through patient stone's thrown love
An arrow shoot
Shot, landing, dove
Plucked from sandy crust
Patience, stone-thrower
Putter-togetherer of things solid
With lathe lather true wet sides
Put up the mantle
Throw up keystone
Carve doorstep, doorway
Make it home

297

AT THE EDGE OF THE FIELD OF STARS

Sky hues are for all times—
A bloodiness of dry dawn
A filtered blue for a skein of fancy
The broad spectral discharge of highest noon
Or broad deeps of plundered *sombras*
But give me placid stellar views
Open the canopies of heaven
And glut this dusky earth with starry night
Tear down penumbral walls between
Here and eternity gritted and mysterious
Darkening plains never touched, cast amongst
Fields filled with life, giving quarter
Beckoning to our well of gravitas

298
Astounded by chasms of wilderness
By the way words slip into song
Keep one aim
Be the clear, ringing witness to life

299
Observe, hold and stay these shaded eyes
Winds have lost the grassed-over tracks
Keep big cat pace, shoulder blades sharp
Mimic the practiced masters

300
ENCOUNTER
With shadows perched
Like wraiths up the
Slope from the east
Came daylight long
By an edge of the stream
Riachuelo narrow,
A hollow drowsing
Stood six hounds
Black, brown, grey
I pulled my lean *pistola*
But they had gone

301
Winding switchbacks, sharp declivities
Declination unknown
Fast ascend to *rapprochement*
'Twixt wisp of spirit and heart of rock

302
Leaf-deluge weather blasts blatant potency
Overpowers turf
A fragile world is out there
Between upside down grey mountains
Inverted electric riverheads

303
Ask for pure preciousness
Spark fluid waves of fire
Crece my within-glow
Boil these massed veins and dilate the pupils

304
Hat band is the string for a bow
Madden the spindle as
Smoke uncoils
Ask for flame from a kindred spirit

305
Ring around the moon
Squaw wood rattles my old boots dry
Wipe away scuffs to reveal new life
Shiny, waxed companions

306
One day on the ranch
Laid bricks patio-style
Baked soft bread
Listened to gathering wind in the palms

307
Weave tall sprigs
Soak them in bitter water
Warp and weave through shadows
Daylight wanes, that fabric of hours

308
The spirit-that-moves-through-all-things
Shelters high-stalked land
Bleeds ocher earth
Silts the running streams

309
Wayward waterfowl
Banded vision
The kingsnake amongst rushes
Uncoils hidden streams

310
Door swings in rising wind
Orion splays above
Wind-blown ghost-lit contrails
Midnight weather’s turning

311
Sniffing with angular snouts
Coyotes read tracks
Speak among themselves in the guttural tongue
Separate vocabularies for the kill

312
Creatures foreign to this earth:
(Not tangled serpents—such wholesome servants)
But minds of great cats, spongiform mushrooms
Molds of magenta and ultraviolet

313
Claptrap coyotes wail
A lot of words bandy about these parts
Around fire's glow I peek at other worlds
The plummy moon just hangs there

314
Grandmother's abandoned hearth stones
Slip to beach sand
Fire-worn wood husks
Smoke the echoing wash

315
What cracked arch is this
Leaning across the land?
What rose-chinked mystic house, this
Crusadic crumble?

316
Pick the loaming up
Weigh massive clay
Streaked with desecration
A deserted humus of epochs

317
On far heights
As worldlights blink
I watch from below
This cup never so warm
This height never so mellow
Beyond ache we go
Shadowed hill do tell
Yet ringing meaning slightly flees
Her dress caught in the brush
And I sit still in mystery

318
Rise, tattered earth-traveller, tremble
The air falls cold and heathen
Scope yonder country wide
Beyond first hearths lies flatland

319
It's time to take the moment to be lost
Revisit loves lost and found
Tame the battered spirit in hands of the great one
Wander 'till soul is safely found

320
O to muse a thousand flaming births
Revers'ed battlefield
Hush the silence
Bombed-out estrellated fields
Ripe dawn draws nigh
Pulverizes cracked *cielo*
Drops magenta pearly rain
Hills swarm in a
Bushland apoco-dawn

321
Let whispers sing
Especially from a lovely mouth
Choose her and only her
Sing those whispers back till found

322
Crazy reflexive contrary cloud
Pink and blue and bubble-headed
Whither thou goest? And why thy gathering
In places unbecoming for rain-dropping?

323
No easy come and even harder went
By mist-torn plateaus
Cries descended depth-plumbed night
Prey is washed away

324
Wending craggy stillness
Towers pierce the sky
Condor sweeps
Condor passes
Atop ridges such and high
'Twere mere meeting vision
Clear and plenty
Cool morning's wash of air
To mountain's turmoil lies
With flick'ring wings
Through swirling fever breath
Disdained envious slow-failing frivolity
Wheels great wings
Condor's passing high

325
A perfect place
Cannot be replicated
Hold the breath
Retreat gently swaying

326
Power on with caffeine
On limber legs unstrung
Scramble in grand arroyos
All days end in upper reaches, ends-of-roads

327
Little bee
Spins into the house
Before I can shut the door
Spend a minute rescuing

328
Then the hoarded secrets
Tided forth
From soaring hills
Sallied washes
Lost rivulets
Cozy hare-rests
Quail tracks
Damp sand
The corner of a sharp-edged pottery shard
Piece of heart
Crumbs of fire
And nothing more
Half a dozen scattered stories
Scattered, pilfered lie

329
Wash stillness from the dawn
Even you
Should feel these dreams immensely
And carry them far

330
Hauntingly shelvingly
Mesmerize-making
Loss heart-stopping
Describes yet decries
Sudden onset of night
The blackest din of unsung thunder might
Heart of cirrus circuses
Heaven-high
Light-spilt plains of airy dry
The penumbral cone
Shape'd wing'ed ornate
Half of earthly delight
Come darkness
Come one, come all
Thus said light to heaven's fall

331
At your side
I forget myself even for death
Gather while the sky is light
Roast long stalks in winter earth

332
Drums along the horizon
Beat the starry dusk
Winds among confuse'd hills
Pulse with arisen mandate

333
Wind of the west
Telegraphy of power
Encilia-on-the-plateau
Wave farewell, sweet present

334
Breathe, mesa-top
In the midnight hour
Creatures inhuman walk
Croon empty land

335
The long-shadowed moon
Rides cottonball clouds
Hunger pangs hide to hills
Please save sufferers harmony

336
A month of cold comes on
Shears warmth like fat
Feed the hungry
And all, no matter, will be well

337
If there be need for water
Let it spring forth
If there be need for beans, gorge
Pray this then, and nothing more

338
One day it shall be
A weak country, crippled, spent like a cartridge
Now a power streams unseen
Lets petals pulse, collapse

339
Desolate peaks stand in the downpouring
Furred denizens curl close
Concentrate in narrow burrows
Escape pale dearth

340
A horrid mystic hearth
Gapes chills of snow
Moans the moon-cry
This beginning year of cold

341
This crinkled map, secure, divine
Holds reckless course through chasms
Gravellous and plighted
Secrets withstand careful observance

342
The track is washed away
A grainy voice
Downcanyon
Beckons

343
Season of *tamiva*; the dry growing time
Cactus seeds shoot forth
Warp to heavens
Embolden Indian time

344
Stars slide faintly by
The careening branches
Tendrilize dawn
Along wide land
Drylands
Sad-song long reaches
Dune place
This spot goes solitarily
With keen sense
Scent of lavender rose
On fire the day
On fire it
Brills so

345
In deep serenity, sleep
For stars reign down and
All night sails
Steers us in a gulf of doldrums

346
Arroyo seco climbing notes
Rimland brims with
Signs of loss and tracks of wet
Earth lies in broken spines

347
Die, illusions of yesterday
Breathe, Spiderwoman, singer of dances
You have freedom to weave songs anew
Camp on the eastern edge of the world

348
The cricket
Has made it this far into dawn country
Celebrating himself
He looks for his girl

349
Each herb has a secret
Feel deeply for it
And come away the wiser
Earth oozes soft advice

350
Give me a high-voiced girl
And open country
Eternal blossoms splay anew
Let roasted rock map the future

351
I ate eggs and bacon at the border
Whoah, I said and burnt rubber in a circle
Surrendered my immortality
Stepped into a hieroglyphed land

352
Welcome a shared *desiderata*
Hear each coyote generation pass
Intent to feed on cats
'Tis an episodic tryst

353
Spoken Nazca languages graft
Diffuse lines in tilled soil
Heed the tumbling rhythm, the
Web of wringing branches

354
Flint strikes wilted sprigs
A spark scurries forth to
Light the eve
A feast of withered branches

355
Ices flash from beetling sky
Cry of the screech owl
These creosote have waited now ten thousand years
Rise, fetid winterscape

356
Slap a round in the chamber
Pull the trigger, hurtle
Tongue of flame upcountry
A shot for the ridges

357
A fold of nocturnal snow settles on the mount
With lemons and a thick-greased skillet
In my hand
I sit by the damp orchard portal

358
White stars, white peak
Cornbread cooks in the grove
My house the first
Beneath broad mountain

359
Walk roads paved with bits of shell
Grind ancient seeds with sandals
Know full well the western Sphinx
Of beaten mountain path

360
Two hats rest on pegs by the door
One is a blue fresh cap
The second a sweat-shored rag
Guess the favorite

361
Thick bubble-meat patties
Sizzle on the skillet
Pour a mash of steam
Wrap in lettuce and black bread

362
The little sapling will block the view
Of the broad peak
Yet water her
She grows surprises

363
Ration the wine tonight
Scarf is set and dawn is far
Morning ice will glaze the leaves
Before we're done

364
Sit under darkened sky with open ears
Night birds nestle
Sing drowsy hymns
In the broad compass of shelter

365
Swath of moon-baked country
On the other side
Poise at earthen berm
Shadows of the owls leap

366
Crème-terra
Fronts of frost
Snow shifts in the crevasse
The white sky loves drifts

367

A NURSERY RHYME

Glass-pressing nose, he knows he goes
Under the hose the fingerly toes
Twenty below and crying 'Aho'
Lubberly hole'dly striking the pose

368

Winter gusts through the clattered defile
Welcome home!
Say hello, sunken bowl
Snow-burnt peaks

369

Pass without leaving a print
Along the wash way
Ride on heads of rock
Feng shui passenger

370

So smooth
So enduring
That only the winds can wonder
Such is the blownwood
He has lain far
Through fits of desert whipping
He has rolled by trails untold
Vistas unforgettable
Basked in turns unbespoken
He now heaves to,
Raggedly tired
Bleached by wanderlust

371
While boiling rich coffee
Bees sing in the hollow
Greensleeves on carved instruments
Christmastide, the first day

372
Be so still that
Even a dune can be airy paradise
Even a glazed stone
A turning world

373
The 6th day of Christmas
Flows from the summit
Frosted forests
March from blackened reaches

374
Christmas morning lies bright and cool
On the land like current
You can smell the turkey basting
Pull on your shoes

375

Pass the thin-soiled fencepost land
Century stalks cantilever and
Cactus sparrows streak through dense shrubs
This land of low-uttered Indian voices
And high-pitched night wind
Guarantees safe passage through
Pale yucca blossoms
Crumbled stone columns
Pink fragments of earth
Wilted springs on thin tap
Land of hearts
Every one touched which passed this way
Ancient highland flats
And bees in the cool morning bottom
Doves at noon
Pass this land then, humming
And pay with twisted reeds
Indwelling natives

376

Elders push pups
Up their scrambled chasm
Rambunctious voices scatter
Soak in precipicial light

377

Reach the soil through a tree
Trace chipped trunk
To tossed earth
Gnarled roots split rock

378
The rabbit leapt out
And I fired, missed
And so enjoyed his leaps
Bounds from the scope

379
White sand and buzzing hills
A dizzying sky
The canteen is a can for chugging
Millennial micro-time

380
A shelving beast
Haunts glowing hills
Sotto voce off-key
Cave of the bird bones

381
Dreams flit fast through deep brush
Leave me here in heaven
Where birds sing long through night
And beetles carve the loam

382
Dust-dining spider mites
Uncurl dead leaves
Pick apart frail spines
Implode the cactus cadaver

383

THE LONG ASCENT

Before sun's urges arose I rose and sortied
Sort of cold but full of meat and hot drink
I rolled eggs in tortilla shreds
And decamped, closed door
Said nothing,
With deep misgiving left
Went
Parlayed silence into movement
Along the wide wash rim
Stumped past trees in undead light
Said goodnight to night
And good morning then
Fell forward into wash bends
Stooped and lay down and got up,
Fear like a wet sock in my mouth
Knowing a slipped foot would finish my leg
Leg on, leg over, a journey like
A thousand miles beginning
Birds—hawks then
Colonies above the plain stood in eyries of bedrock
I climbed
Bating breath with heart beat out of me
Hand over fist
Fist over knuckles
On the high-rocked land

384

Chocolate-heaped spring
First of the days
Salt-sugar and grey honey
Melt in the crystal canyon

385
BELL STONE
Once on mountain rambles
I came across a sandy plain
Amongst baked boulder fields
Wondering what it was
I wandered in
And found a stone
Tall, great, grandly
Placed at true center
With white sand all around
Heat rising
Flies buzzing
I struck it with my fist
And clear sound rang
Like orange bells
Templed sun dial
Simple, clean, dear
I, nodding
Backed away
And left it standing there

386
Gather *datura* with sticky fingers
The spider moon swings overhead
Dance with the coming-of-age
Beat earth in a circular route

387
Awoken by the wind
A bleak birthday dawn
Storm moves in and
Thrashes palm tidings

388

I can't be killed because I know how to suffer
Everything happens for a reason
Everything has its own place
I hold my place on this mesa
And death does not approach
Keeps wary distance, circling
Shudders hungrily at bay

389

THE HACKING CREATURE

Beware, beware the sharp hill's crown
Four went up and raced their way down—
The hacking creature terrified us
But we gathered strength to search
Atop the ranch's lone pinnacle
With hearts in our mouths we climbed
The sudden silence stunned us
The more so because we were young
Hadn't the creature been calling?
So we peeled away in terror
I frantically ran in the rear
The hacking creature is still out there
Perhaps it's a fox or a rodent
But not to be trifled with
Do not use its name in vain
Where is it now? It could even be
Resting behind the toilet seat
Or in the closet, waiting to pounce
Most likely, it will live on in imagination
And haunt dreams of future ones
So beware, beware the hacking creature
We prefer to leave it at leisure

390
Along the 500-year trail
Sand has washed from boulders
On the straight, high path
Barrel cacti block the way

391
Along the lean path
Collect pungent herbs of night
Where did autumn go?

392
Below a pale moon
We sortie from shadowed rooks
Feed in clouds of bugs

393
Crazed violins play the earth's turning
Doves coo in the eve
A setting sun irradiates
Soft rain on the summit

394
Desert mounts once were capped with snow
Now a tangled breeze blows loosely in
Capsized trees stray roots in air
A dry melody of downfall

395
This, a body lost to ash
A ribcage left in light to dry
Femurs, thorax, temple-down
A sticky offering to wind

396
Flying far from water
They gab on tops of trees
High branches bend ever so slightly
From crowns they flee for home

397
HOMECOMING
Set forth today at day's bright edge
A fellow creature strolled the way
Coyote, I said, come see me
But he sped along the road
Like a rocket run
My tires crunched leaves and tired
The capped range drew down
And under the Thanksgiving tree
Ills flowed out
I curled up at last
Coyote hid gently
And sent commiserations

398
The twinkling honk-world lies thither
Yet these slopes are guarded well
Open the petals of secrets
Feel out the names of gourds

399
Cry through fields of cactus
Rub peppers in the eyes
Loss lies sharp-set
Among bitter wandered hills

400
Travel alone beyond the headlights
There, a panting figure stoops
Bates his breath to snatch some bread
This is where our two natures meet

401
Stay the hand that strays to pick a bloom
Laugh at an injudicious time
A wild wind wipes sorrow from the sky
But cannot forget me of you

402
Bathe in the sound of waters
Scoop from the spring so sweet
Not all hours pool in our basins
We cannot drink a whole stream

403
A long light holds on furthest ridge
And even though we don't see
Or understand what is there
Forms wheel amidst the shadows

404
Rockstone egg
Shaped of rolled dough
Clammed hammering
Resounding bleakly
Mote-of-a-pile
Somehow came to rest
Like a beggar poised alone
Guess where you fell
Or what befell
Within the honored hall
Smack in the dry bed
Like a gargoyle's hunched shoulders

405
The oracle looped away through stones
Swung a backward glance
'*C'est une vérité, petit prince*
My truth is universal'

406
Blown leaves cross before
A wind-whipped shore
Sunlit drops come lacing down
To freshen them the more

407
Glazed light looms low
And from the south rolls thunder
Bands of earth cloud-shaded lie
Along the storm-thrashed route

408
Tops of trees blow in dissolute light
Highlands bathe in shadow
Devils dance the dusk in
The wild orb slips from rocky waves

409
Time drums in holy deeps
Sleeping circles ring the shore
Churn the quicksand to find silver
A caved beach spills bleached bones

410
Time of the beekeeper moon
The frenetic sky swarms
Honey drizzles from heaven
Drips through atmospheres

411
As I wait for the kettle to boil
I add stones to my fireplace
Set at sandy point
The pot boils over and the cup runneth over

412
Scribble on a page through grease
Below the dusk go low cries
Peeled notes curl in damp firelight
'The people' pass lightly by

413
Be thankful for what is given
A corner of cloud pegs the moon
Free wine courses the veins
Let the world dream on!

414
I crept under palm rows
Squeezed streams from deep humus
Slept in muddy elbows
As mosquitoes whispered at my ear

415
Springtime; plush fields hide succulents
Woodpeckers ply the snags
And come away with green worms
Soft feasts of jelly

416
Derive unbearable pleasure
From fresh rain
Crouch low
The soaked land smells of cinnamon

417
How long has it been
Since we sped to world's end?
Where are you, lost in the great south?
And where am I for letting you go?

418
I am a sailor on the purple sea
Bésame, chica mia
Let me taste your foam
Your undulating waves
Déjame dormir en tus brazos
We will navigate together
Hasta bajamos abajo las estrellitas del sur

419
The foreign words rolled off my tongue
And now I speak English a parrot
Squawking the meaning
My mind has settled in far country

420
Diesel lingers on the dusty track
In an orange-peel sunset
Layers of crickets occlude
The perigee moon

421
Lights dazzle wet streets
Broad leaves ring the moon
My pencil traces air
A long path south to you
Sirena of the broken sea
Swim from boiling water
Those lamps eat moths
I, too, am engulfed

422
My land is a spiny corpse
It walks with one arm upraised, points through narrows and broad reaches
Ravens half-fold their wings and frown to burn out eyes
I feel my way out impaled forests, dilapidated thunderheads

423
Distill cactus blossoms to resin
And night flowered kisses to ale
Trail fingers through drifting cobwebs
Drink *mescal* from quails' nests

424
Black beetles twirl
And hide fern trailings away
What earthen letters could spell
Myriad insect paths?

425
I slapped the little fly
And he came apart in wings
Flew into death's country
So is that what it is to die?

426
SUMMER STORM
PART ONE
And then it came like tornadoes
Water sweet
Life playing
Draining awash
Removed it so
Replaced it did dry wounds
Tossed water ran
Hunted cracks
Chimney-stone foundations
Riverbed channels
A careering tepid drench
Wetted smoky soil
Altered foundations
The once-per-annum
Year's spent searching
Earth's careening
At last splurging,
August's sweet spot
Wildly found

PART TWO
I kept awake all night
With the light flashing
Overbearance passing
Window panes rattled
Hardscrabble removed
Dribbled, splattered
Upended and returned in
Revolutions of heaven
Yet there I stood
Not unlike a small animal defenseless
But convinced of eventual passing

427
Choquechaca, siete culebras
Quetzalcoatl rose from the East
Yet lost all power in dusty realms
These lands of crow and beast

428
Leathern helmets rot away
In a secret Damascene soil
A silver spoon bleeds life
By the reed-crept well

429
Farthest back in narrow hills
An elephant tree sleeps softly
Droops its mighty boughs
Awaiting vanished pickers

430
At bluff's bottom rests
A half-buried kettle
Chairs rot where they lie
The 20-year meal swept downwash

431
I brushed the side of a cactus
And revelled in the making of things
Thorn's spare form
Such joy in small design

432
Sitting before the range
I realized I was free
And soon unwound declining trails
Trod fragrant blushing mazes

433
The venerable old stone
With its pockmarked back
Guards the lip
Of the fluid wash

434
Sight a rock duck
This white man stone
Points the wrong way
Others are less obtrusive

435
The sea dried away in the wink of an eye
And the people who asked
What was under the waters
Were left with dry answers

436
Wild America
Grows a great feast, a
Green spread rediscovered
Matchless in dawning immensity

437
The timid old can
Hides in the briers
He had been laced
By a hundred bullets

438
Tree frogs whirr as the
Pungent eve settles
Here by the berm, the
First field from the mount

439
High clouds brush the eve
And although unexpected
A storm is on its way
Contours flee before it

440
Conversations on the mount
I speak to the spirits
Laugh to calm them down
They fear I've come to steal

441
Yonder agave turns human
Stands in waning light
A forlorn hunchback
Grim against dusky embers

442
With a face full of smoke
And a cup in the coals
Fling sand on the fire
A feral wind has risen

443
I wake with a stomach full of hunger
Where am—but wait
This is a wild garden
Overgrown in the clouds

444
Grainy sand drifts
Thick upon the peak
Twisted agave knives
Hide dry sheep prints

445
In the backcountry
Learn to love oatmeal
Mixed with flakes of chocolate
Mixed with dregs of tea

446
Under the alpine massif rests an
Airy *albergue* of molten lavender
Ocher falls
Streak the Guadalupe Trail

447
I heard voices in the wind
And so asked them
With neighborly goodwill
Déjame pasar

448
Clambered country is too rough
So drowse prettily away
Swim effortlessly through peaks
In dreams of gilded night

449
After a hard day's journey
I reach the top bluff
The clean trail lies waiting
I ask 'Where were you before?'

450
A hat crown crosses the canyon rim
And I, naked
Drip-drying after bathing
Flee like a wild animal

451
By the swollen creek
Oats cook under the cottonwoods
I, busy, stir them with a branch
Chew gummy grain

452
Quail wail the hour
Under a torpid moonrise
How should they know
The distance dawn must pace?

453
Every canyon has a lover
Even the craggy drop
Keeps a human keeper
A lonely helper in the wild

454
The path ahead lies
Unmarked
And I shall only pass
With a promise to return

455
We cling to wizened tomes
Yet breathing upcountry, free
Find agave pages real
So read from living volumes

456
Hay un refugio
Este lado de la cumbre
Una casa dorada
En humo nublado

457
Ringing silence
Ears send old sounds mind's way
'Listen to this then, friend'
Burns *pureza* in circles of thought

458
Birds sing the moon up
Pick through plush sprigs
I'm finally home
To write by lumined light

459
History is a host of friends
Past generations point the way
Leave *bella* notes in buried trails
'Go here, not there' they say

460
With cholla in his fleshy palm
By hand and teeth unzipped the pack
Swabbed iodine and dripped it dry
Wound black wound with gauze

461
What madness it has been
To fall so far for you
No bottom rushes up to meet me
I pass the center of the earth

462
Working my way down
From cliffhung vaults
I spot a sly footprint
Left over from time

463
Leaves like birds rise
Something uncurls in the mesquite
Shadow-play, unknown
Bracken great-nest

464
Chew fat off the littlest bones
Of an upland quail
Its pot-roasted feet
Keep rice dregs warm

465
Bugs chew broad leaves
Scramble through
A miniature forest
Blue petals and spined cadavers

466
Hummingbird watches me
Through the tangle
She isn't sure what to do
Spins closer

467
Creosote tea oils
Float on the surface
A bitter taste
For a simple mug

468
The centipede, lost
Follows the brick's edge
The sun downs
He takes the winding way

469
There are ghosts on the roads
It is the witching hour
The darkness a frothy opal
Who are we to fly on steeds of night?

470
Tea in the shadowed window
A cloudy wind sweeps by
Brashly whips all to dust
Yellow blossoms float through spring

471
Here I come, crashing through lavender
The wild wind rises
It knows I'm close
To the peak

472
The huntress lands on wings of stone
She's too big to reach the nest
Parents cry alarm
And spin to make a scene

473
The pack laughs it up
At the entrance to the cove
They'll roam long this eve
Powered on far-ranging humor

474
The bird-orchestra chortles
And a roadrunner purrs
Stay still
Primeval music requires rapt audience

475
The air fills with dust
Un sabor colorado
Rastro tan venenoso
Sunset, burning sunset

476
Into happy ages
Children of the night
Shall speed rocky gulfs
And sing to evening stars

477
Mid-spring and
Bugs cover lamps
Seek hot bulbs
Fall with flailing wings

478
Spring surrounds like a warm glove
Crickets shrill from homely limbs
Shadows grow short
The animal host reveals its face

479
Then with unbinding wings
She came to earth
Unbridled crow claws
Scattered dead straw

480
Unearth glorious excelsior graves
Free tracks melt with age
Withdraw from this inhuman place
Of scattened bones

481
The molted Golden Eagle
Is a discriminating
Wild-eyed
Bloody-minded sophisticate

482
Give me the grey desert bee
With the sting of a pin
A nose for sweet flowers
A miniature noon traveller

483
Old desert road
Lies ramshackle-run
Muscles ache to run
But this is snake time

484
VIENEN LOS CONQUISTADORES
They came tramping
To scatter upland game
Their game the reaching
From *España* to crumbled mesas
Hawks and eagles played
In their draggled Moorish hair
Swords rusted in winding reaches
For want of battle
Adios, complacencia
They stepped out, spat
Sank up to their knees in sand

485
Earth creaks as it turns
Go hand over hand
Frenetically higher
To gather the vista

486
Slowly, slowly
The bug's antennae
Come out from under the leaf
Waving this way and that

487
The battered old pan
Fills with jellied blood
Poor fallen jackrabbit
I had been quicker

488
With waning strength
Follow twisted, rocky path
It is easier to continue
Than go back

489
366 days on the land
Light plays on the stream bottom
The gamekeeper of *salvatierra total*
Hatches ancient seeds

490
Draw with a rasp
A final breath
Sketch for future friends
Star charts in loops of sand

491

LORD OF THE RANGE

How much I wish to show you
Cannot be imagined
Take paltry steps
Along my rich road
This is wild country
And I am King
Thorn-crowned Lord of the Range
Alive for holy song
You, bright eyed maiden
Must visit this sundered realm
Wash yourself in August rain
Burn hot with dawn
I play the flute for you to follow
With wild hair, trusting me
I am the starry ceiling
The beak'ed bird dance
Surrender and follow
Or all is lost
And I resume pacing
A ghost in the sands
An emperor of silent dunes
Here I am
There you stand
Step forward
Show yourself the queen

492

Blessed are those
Who work the land
The beetled
Yellow earth

493
A single meteor shoots away
Sheds splintered trail
Down southern sky
Am I its only witness?

494
A blackbird
White-breasted
Greets the dawn
From highest branches

495
CHUPACABRA
One night I awoke as a *chupacabra*
And startled, smelled everything
Found my skin grown to leather
My eyes complex lenses
Consciousness overturned and
I walked without thinking of 'in' or 'out'
'Past' or 'present'
I haunted stunted forests
And fields filled with plastic
I ran the highlands
And feasted on entrails
Mosquitoes bit my ears
I itched with fleas
In my thirst I trusted to fortuitous circumstance
Lapped stale waters
My heart beat slowly and
My voice cried of its own volition
Strange flesh hung from my bones
I hungered to touch the moon
To drink nectar from the night

496
Under slow moon
Waltz the night away
Lay votives by water's edge
Brass bull frogs sing accompaniment

497
Burn bent incense on the wind
In the *Casa de Cuerva*
Hand over this high-mourned place
To grizzled, lustrous creatures

498
Sleep like a babe
In the clutch of mountains
Your hair the grass
Blown by starry breath

499
MARCH OF THE CHOLLA
One night, upon a darkened ridge
Above a blazing valley
A feral cactus field set out
To take back human lands
They'd waited long for a new era
Upon twisted airy heights
Waited for days gentle to come
The peace of native hands
But wayward two-legg'ed beasts came
Tore up fields and fallow ground
Made off with earth's good riches
Struck skies through with sound

And man-made stars whined overhead
Not knowing where to turn
The cholla chiefs spoke all together
'We'll make the humans learn
They darken skies with smoggy scum
And suck up all our water
Each day we wait more earth becomes
A trap for our own slaughter
They have a master plan in place
To squeeze out all the gold
Their greed shall kill our living race
So we must act, the bold
We elders know, eons before
Dark peoples walked our ways
They picked and chose amongst our spines
Like wise customers who paid
With their own blood they gave us life
And combed our birds' nest hair
In these lean days earth shakes with strife
High hawks cry out despair
To war, my fellow fallow beings!
Let not a day go by
Until these humans grow new wings
As if the pigs could fly
For flying far from here they'd help
To vanish far from sight
We, as earth's new rootless masters
Shall set these slights aright
Make everything as was before
And all of us shall sing
Those humans, they shall be no more
And nature, again, the king'
The chiefs raised high and soaring voice
'To war, happy hoard, to war'
And out from ledges set with brush
Marched cholla toward the floor
One chief shouted up to stars beyond
Cried to pale moon over-risen
'Follow me, my friends, and find reward
In tasting the forbidden!
What if Eve had not tasted Apple

What if Apple had tasted Eve?'
One day, and then the next
From the west all toward the east
The rowdy forest swept
Left mountains dark with green
Became a ferocious army
Slackly moving toward their thirst
And after vaulting gullies
They came to house and hearth
Far afield lay a fire pit
With blown ash mixed with dirt
A boy sat and watched them come
They were an ugly, angry herd
'We now are men' the cholla cried
Raised torches in the ranks
The boy fixed back a broken glare, said
'It's not all that you might think
For coming down from mountaintop
Your freedom lies up there
The longer that you dally here
Is the greater that you dare
You wish to be us humans then?
So tell me that you care—
Why place your hopes in mimicry
When all there was to us
Was dreaming dreams that could not be
And building for the dust?
To be a human, now you know
Is to be cast aside
I'd rather live a simple life
Below those skies so wide
All life on earth fears us, beware
We live in banishment
Turn round now and homeward fare
Avoid fate most imminent
Go back before you turn like us
Go, share your love around
Feel earth and water, sun and shade
Put roots back in the ground
Go now, please now, my newfound friends
Before your magic fades'

The cholla chiefs spoke loud, then low
And raised their hands to choose
And so they voted to return
To where the sun played through
The last chief raised his voice to call
As the cholla all marched out
'Take care, young boy' the cactus wished
From the middle of the rout
'There's things yet for you to see, my child
A plan in this world's plot
It's not that every animal
Can be something it's not
It's not that every wild thing
Can be so pleased to be
A steward of the low spots, a
Gamekeeper for the trees, a
Cloud keeper of supernature
In your science of the air
One day, you'll see, humans shall lead
And make all right, don't fear
Wild creatures need man, too, you know
On you we could depend
And till the magic for you begins
You've won a heartfelt friend'
Then all the cholla left the boy
And the army disappeared
And where before a troupe had stood
The day's dark light shone weird
The boy leant out and saw a spot
Of something red like blood
He reached and plucked from dusty tide
A fragile cactus bud
It had fallen, unbeknownst
From the chieftain's good sharp crown
The boy, he took it in his palm
He sniffed and turned it round
Then wove it carefully in his hair
Like a bloody bless'ed nugget
And he felt a change in air
Before he knew what happened
Before the birds could nest

An eclipse washed down upon the land
Then vanished like a breath
And so from deep foundations
All humans came to him
People shook with happy cries
And found awareness deep within
It was a sea change with no ending
A beginning lost in time
A science of photosynthesis
A tide of moleculic rhyme
Humans found their voice again
It came from lungs of wind
And darkened shadows moved on ridges
These cholla were now friends
Towers lost to time stood still
Then caved inward to dust
Eve bit her apple for renewal
And sank her teeth in lust
She spoke clear words to the cholla
They stood planted by her hand
'Together we have joy, and
With you we make our stand
So now you stand awaiting, friends
Patient in the wild
A new day rises, dawn bleeds hot
Earth shall not be defiled
We bury civilization's rot
By this apple core I promise
Peace from hill to hill and dale
Protection from the comets'
And all the crazed lost species
Of a world in sharp decline
Rose up with voices singing
For this conscious lady fine
For what animal like humans
Could reach out and touch the stars
With fiery dance and shining tools
Part Venus and part Mars?
So beings came from oceans blue
And the Arctic's dying rays
To see and hear the sudden truth

Of Eve's new wakeful days
Then she did end her apple
And shared it with a snake
Lifted voice above the crowd
And then pure words she spake
'I am your young and lucid queen
Of man and world alike
Let's together drink from sparkled stream
And set the world in light'

500
Faucets drip in the aching *barrio*
And a pale orb floats above
Somewhere, thunder rolls across distant plains
Crickets echo in the empty house

501
As many poems as days in the life
Blessed girls and boys give to receive
Pass then this struggle in barren hinterlands
These sliding tests swing briefly by

ABOUT THE AUTHOR

Ethan grew up on a ranch near Thermal, California. He is a graduate of the Idyllwild Arts Academy and Bennington College in Vermont. Seeking adventure, he moved to Cuzco, Peru where he travelled the Andes and read Neruda. Now 29, he is a graduate student in Latin American security policy at the Monterey Institute of International Studies.

www.ingramcontent.com/pod-product-compliance
Ingram Content Group UK Ltd.
Pitfield, Milton Keynes, MK11 3LW, UK
UKHW020128250726
13967UKWH00002B/544